Interview Skills:
How to Get Hired NOW!
Quick Job Interview
Success Tips

Dr. Angela D. Massey

A Gap Closer™ Publication

Interview Skills:
How to Get Hired NOW!
Quick Job Interview
Success Tips

A Gap Closer™ Publication
A Division of Life On Purpose Publishing

ISBN: 0-9729250-1-5
ISBN-13: 978-0-9729250-1-3

This publication is designed to provide accurate and authoritative information in regard to the subject matter covered. It is sold with the understanding that the publisher is not engaged in rendering legal or other professional service. If legal advice or other expert assistance is required, the services of a competent professional person should be sought.

—From a declaration of principles jointly adopted by a committee of the American Bar Association and a committee of publishers.

Cover Design © 2012 by Dr. Angela D. Massey

DEDICATION

To Sarah E. Ellis: Thank you for your diligence and commitment to following the steps. You say I helped you make some important decisions when we worked on your job exit strategy. The truth is, you helped me realize that helping others realize their potential is my purpose, and putting it into words in the form of this book is my duty.

Rock on, Sarah!

CONTENTS

AUTHOR'S INTRODUCTION

Congratulations! The company to which you have applied has looked favorably on your application; now they want *you* to come in for an interview. That's why now is the time to make sure *you* are 100% prepared to get *that* job.

Research suggests almost 85% of working adults interview, on average, five times before being hired for their current position. Successful interviewing skills, when properly applied, will greatly increase your chances of getting the job you want. This guide will give you the information you need to interview with confidence.

Face it: You are responsible for letting your potential employer know what makes you the more qualified candidate. Competition among candidates requires companies to find the best person for the job. Since your potential employer is faced with the task of deciding who is the best fit for the job, your skills and abilities must stand out so that you can get the job. They have to know *what's in it for them* (WIIFT) if they hire you. To prepare to give your potential employer what she wants, it is critical that you know the ins and outs of giving an outstanding interview. So sit back and get ready to take some notes so that *you* can get *that* job!

Happy Interviewing!

Dr. Angela D. Massey
Windsor, Connecticut

HOW TO USE THIS GUIDE

In today's economic environment finding a job is a full-time job! Undoubtedly, you've been searching the Internet looking for tips, tricks, and strategies to help you gain an edge over all the other job-seekers in your field. Your search has led you to this guide.

I know you're busy. You don't have two or three extra hours to read through a 250 page book, so I purposely wrote this guide to be short and to the point! To help you maximize your time, the first chapter of this guide *(The Quick and Dirty Version: Summary Upfront)* is a summary of what is in each subsequent chapter—the tips! Once you have read through the summary information, you can go to each corresponding chapter for more details.

Additionally, I have included an extensive list of employment related websites in the Appendix. I've done all the work for you! The list—the best of the best—is categorized in the typical sequential steps job-seekers should take: Resumes, Cover Letters, Interviewing, and Thank-You Letters/Notes. *Please note at the time of this publication, all links worked. If you try a link and it does not work, let me know so that I can update the list.* Enjoy!

1 THE QUICK & DIRTY VERSION: SUMMARY UPFRONT

What Are Employers Looking For?

1. Employers are looking for candidates with high emotional intelligence, knowledge-based skills, and transferable or portable skills.
2. Communication skills (listening, verbal, and written) account for 80% of most jobs. Technical skills account for only 20% of a job.
3. It is important that you are strong in eight key areas: problem-solving, leadership, organizational skills, outstanding communication skills, customer service skills, time management, project management, and critical thinking.

Two Agendas

1. Your agenda of getting the job is more important than the interviewer's agenda of hiring a suitable candidate.
2. If you remember that your agenda is the most important agenda you can focus on your qualifications and strengths as you prepare for the interview.
3. Think of yourself as a consultant there to help the organization become better.

INTERVIEW SKILLS: HOW TO GET HIRED NOW!

Mental Preparation

1. You must use the power of your mind to program yourself for a successful interview.
2. Knowing why you want the job will give you the confidence you need when you interview.
3. Using written and verbal affirmations are the quickest methods to program yourself for success.
4. If you are going to be successful you must believe in your ability to succeed, and act as if you have what you want before you get it.
5. Take the time to mentally prepare for your interview; it is one of the most important parts of the process.

Physical Preparation

1. Thoroughly research the company so that you can develop a mental snapshot of who they are and what they do.
2. Pay attention to your physical appearance. Whether you are a man or a woman, remember: be clean, be conservative, be free, and be professional.
3. Use your common-sense when it comes to interviews.
4. Prepare a script based on your resume to highlight your competencies.
5. Use the AIDA formula to develop your own Unique Selling Proposition.
6. Participate in a mock interview to prepare for your big day. Plan to spend at least two to three hours in your mock interview.

Now That You're In

1. You can make a good impression if you improve your non-verbal communication skills.
2. The non-verbal communications you should focus on improving are listening, tone of voice, and body language.
3. Use your comprehensive resume as a guide so that you can elaborate on key points.
4. Don't be afraid to toot your own horn!
5. Analyze your work background—even if you believe there are deficiencies—and put an optimistic twist on it.

INTERVIEW SKILLS: HOW TO GET HIRED NOW!

The Nuts and Bolts of the Interview

1. How you answer the job interview questions will determine if you get the job.
2. It pays to be prepared, especially for the competency-based questions designed to ascertain your emotional intelligence.
3. There are, at minimum, 11 standard interview questions you can expect the interviewer to ask.

Emotional Intelligence Questions

1. Emotional intelligence-based questions assess your self-awareness, that is, how well you know yourself.
2. The interviewer may ask questions to determine how well you work with others.
3. Your answers to emotional intelligence-based questions will make the difference in your interview.

Questions You May Ask

1. Be prepared to ask the interviewer a few questions to demonstrate your interest in the position as well as the company.
2. Ask questions to show you were paying attention.
3. Ask questions to demonstrate you know something about the organization.
4. Ask questions to position yourself as a valuable future member of the team.
5. Asking questions can help to increase your likeability factor.

Duh...How to Get Un-stumped If You Get Stumped By a Question

1. There are three problematic areas associated with interview questions: being asked an off-the-wall question, experiencing a momentary memory lapse and becoming speechless.
2. The off-the-wall question is designed to see how fast you think on your feet, to test your problem-solving abilities, and to determine if you can think outside the lines.
3. The best way to handle the momentary memory lapse is to take a notepad and pen so that you can take notes.

4. If you become speechless, ask the interviewer to explain the question so that you can get an idea of what he is looking for.
5. When all else fails, take a sip of water so that you can collect yourself and formulate a response.

What's Next?

1. Summarize your strengths and remind the interviewer that you are the person for the job.
2. Thank the interviewer for his time and consideration of you as a job candidate.
3. Write a thank-you note and send it within eight hours.

2 WHAT ARE EMPLOYERS LOOKING FOR?

So, what are employers looking for? Most Human Resource professionals agree that employers assess potential employees in three areas: emotional intelligence, knowledge-based skills, and transferable or portable skills.

Emotional Intelligence: In 1930, it was called "social intelligence" defined as the ability to get along with other people. By 1985, the same concept was called "emotional intelligence." Popularized by Daniel Goleman's work in 1995, emotional intelligence is defined as the ability to perceive control, and evaluate emotions. You may not recognize the phrase, but you will surely recognize the types of questions it produces: "Tell me about a time when you...." Usually EI-type questions can make interviewees uncomfortable because they don't know what the interviewer wants to hear. I go into great detail in my up-coming book *Interview Questions: How to Answer CORRECTLY!* to help you prepare for these EI-type questions. How you display your emotional intelligence will set the tone for the balance of the interview and will determine if you get the job.

Knowledge-based skills: So what do you know? What skills have you learned from previous jobs, college courses, and life? Knowledge-based skills come from things you've learned. For example, you may have learned how to be more assertive when you attended an assertiveness training seminar. Let me put a sidebar here: Don't take your seminar and past training attendance lightly! Every seminar you attend sends the message that you are serious about improving yourself and your skills.

I'm sure you know this, but I will say it anyway: Your resume should include your formal education, and any training you've received through seminars, webinars, teleseminars, books, audio programs, etc. Your potential employer wants to know what you've done to enhance your expertise. Again, remember, your list of knowledge-based skills should include hard (technical) and soft (communication) skills, marketing or managerial knowledge, product development, etc. Any course that includes a certificate of achievement, a diploma, or a degree should be listed on your resume and in your LinkedIn profile. Additionally, be prepared to talk about what you learned from those classes and how that knowledge translates into a marketable skill.

Transferable or portable skills: All skills, be they knowledge-based or not, are transferable. Think of them as portable skills you always take with you to any job. Your potential employer is interested in your transferable or portable skills, which prompts the question: "What could you offer the company?" Here's what they are looking for—quality employees that possess these eight employable characteristics:

- Problem solving skills
- Leadership skills
- Organizational skills
- Excellent written and verbal communication skills
- Customer service skills
- Effective time management skills
- Project management skills
- Critical thinking skills

According to Drs. Katharine and Randall Hansen of Quintcareers.com, "Successful communication is critical in business." This fundamental skill accounts for 80% of what employers are looking for; in other words, employers are paying close attention to how well you speak, write, and listen. The Hansens list communication skills (listening, verbal, and written) as the *number one critical employability skill* demanded of job seekers. It cannot be expressed strongly enough that you must have excellent portable skills, especially communication skills.

If you fall short in this area, your chances of getting the job just dropped to zero! I advise you to invest in any courses, e-books, seminars, webinars, etc., that you can to develop and improve this critical skill.

3 TWO AGENDAS

Every day that a job goes unfilled costs companies hundreds, if not thousands of dollars. The pressure to fill the position is great because—to use an old adage—time is money. Consequently, there are two agendas in an interview situation: the agenda of the person interviewing you and your agenda.

The interviewer needs to make a decision that will allow her company to go forward. She also wants to hire someone so that she can regain the much needed freedom to get back to her own work. Interviewing is a time-consuming process. For every interview she conducts, another work-related project either goes undone or postponed. She's hoping *you* will be the candidate that will bring the job search to an end.

On the other hand, *you*, the interviewee, need to work—you need the job; that is your agenda. Therefore, yours is the stronger agenda. Capitalize on this strength, and concentrate on what you're bringing to the table—your outstanding qualifications and work experience. Remember, you have no reason to feel intimidated! Career and Life Coach, Susan Britton Whitcomb, suggests: "Think of yourself as a consultant who is there to explore how you can bring value to the organization."

The remainder of this guide will help you successfully advance your agenda by gaining a thorough understanding of the importance of mental and physical preparation. We shall examine each in detail, and I will pass on some valuable tips to help you mentally and physically prepare for your interview.

4 MENTAL PREPARATION

Many years of reading self-improvement books have helped me to better understand human beings and how the mind works. I read somewhere that the mind is like a human computer. Check out these interesting tidbits I discovered during my research for this book that clearly substantiate my case:

- Doctors and scientists now firmly believe that 75% of all sickness and disease starts in the mind.
- Researchers have also proven that stress, which starts in the mind, is the number one cause of all fatigue and illness.
- Some scientists believe we only use 10% of our mind, and the remaining 90% is misused. Therefore, 10% of our mind is causing 75% of all sickness—and we are not even using that 10% properly!
- Researchers have also proven that people who have a healthy and positive attitude—or incorporate positive thinking—live better lives.

How does our attitude affect our lives? When we know how to use the power of our minds to work for us, we can create whatever state of mind we desire. However, most of us fail miserably at getting our minds to work for us. When we go through life on autopilot our minds work against us and create things that, on the conscious level, we don't really want.

There is a proverb that states: "For as a man thinketh in his heart, so is he." Everything starts in your mind! You are what you think you are. Your mind creates everything in your life, and this includes the good and the bad.

I have learned that the subconscious mind, the part of you and me that goes to work to help us get whatever we want—positive or negative—can be controlled. Aha! Why not program yourself to get the job that you want? I'm going to show you how to do just that.

Before we get to the process of mental programming, please take a few minutes to participate in the following exercise. In the first part of this mental programming you will need a pad and pencil, or you can use your computer.

I'm going to assume that your short-range goal is to get the job, that's why you're reading this book; right? If you know why you're doing something, you're much more likely to do it. So, take the next few minutes to do the following exercise. Write and complete each of the sentences below:

I applied for this job because (*fill in the blank*).
I am willing to give up (*fill in the blank*) to be successful in getting this job.
I want this particular job because (*fill in the blank*).
When I get the job, I will feel (*fill in the blank*).

Once you dig inside your own mind to connect with your why, with what you're willing to give up to get your why, and how you want to feel once your why has been accomplished, you will find that staying on tasks and doing the work will be easier.

When consulting with my clients I suggest two powerful aids: written affirmations and vocal affirmations to reinforce their goals. I am suggesting the same to you. It is critical that you learn to think and speak success words. Successful people are keenly aware of how much their words influence their lives.

First, to strengthen your resolve to get the job, learn how to use written affirmations. One of the best ways to create change is by using affirmations. Affirmations are simple statements you say to yourself over and over again. Through constant repetition your subconscious mind absorbs the message and you start taking action to create change. It is a way of changing behavior to achieve your goal. Affirmations create positive thinking—which leads to greater change.

The trick to using effective affirmations is to keep them short and powerful. On 3x5 index cards, preferably different colored ones, write a few affirmations that deal specifically with interviewing well, communicating effectively, having your resume chosen over all others, and the mother of all affirmations—getting the job! You can handwrite or type them, and then cut and paste them onto your cards. I am using a powerful program called Dream Manifestation Wizard that allows me to place my affirmations directly on my computer. I've included a link for you in the Appendix. Here a few of my favorite affirmations:

- I have strong skills.
- I dissolve all distractions to getting this job right now.
- My emotions allow me to concentrate effectively during the interview.
- I focus my attention when I interview.
- Employers want to hire me now.
- I am magnetically drawn to the job that's right for me.
- I am excited and happy to receive the job offer.
- I love the way I feel when I receive the job offer.
- My job search is fruitful.
- I have this job!
- I am the right person for this job.
- This job is mine.

Since your mind is so powerful, yet so unused, doesn't it make sense to feed it positive programming? In fact, check out this great website: http://www.thinkrightnow.com. It is dedicated to helping us maintain a positive attitude. Mike Brescia, the owner, also has an awesome software program that flashes subliminal suggestions in the background while you're working on other things. Believe me, it works!

Second, the next part of the affirmation process is vocal affirmations. You can use some of the great affirmations from http://www.thinkrightnow.com or you can create your own. Here is what I do to incorporate written and vocal affirmations. Feel free to make your own.

I use soft classical music as a background and make a 30-minute MP3 recording of myself speaking my affirmations. Then, with my less than $60 buck Olympus Digital Voice Recorder, I listen to these affirmations every night as I drift off to sleep. This has proven to be one of the most powerful ways for me to program myself for any type of success.

Why not take some time right now to write some affirmations regarding your interview and job-seeking process? You can use the ones I've included. Again, feel free to copy them word for word, or make up your own. Just remember effective affirmations should be short and written in a positive tone. In other words, you don't want to write an affirmation that says: "I am not a smoker" or "I am no longer fat and out of shape." There's some tricky mechanism in our subconscious that completely blows past the word "not," so what it actually hears is this: "I am a smoker" and "I am fat and out of shape." Better affirmations would be: "I am free from tobacco" and "I am slim, trim, and physically fit." Got it?

Mike Dooly, noted author and expert on the law of attraction says thoughts become things! Remember, it matters what you are thinking about yourself and your chances of getting the job you want. Here are three additional steps to assist you in mentally preparing yourself for the interview:

Believe in your ability to succeed. Without sounding too esoteric or mystical, I encourage you to examine your beliefs regarding your ability to get this job.

1. *Do you believe you can do the job?*
2. *Do you believe you deserve the job?*
3. *Do you believe you are qualified for the job?*

Positive self-belief is critical. Believe that success is something you can and will achieve. If you do not believe it, who will? Remember, *belief comes from within and manifests itself without.*

Act as if. Create a mental picture of what it would feel like to go through the interview process, and then get the job offer. One of my coaching clients, Anthony, came to me in dire straits. A single dad of a 2-year-old, Anthony had been looking for a job for almost six months when he consulted with me. His bills were overdue. He was facing an eviction notice, and surviving on the monetary support of family members and government assistance.

Anthony didn't realize it, but his mental attitude was extremely negative and victim-focused. He confessed that because he was so depressed about being unemployed he had started to sleep late every day. He didn't get his job hunt started until noon—a sure sign of apathy!

I advised him to get up every day for a week at 7 a.m., to get dressed as though he had a job, and to act like he had a job while he was searching the Internet and other sources looking for one. Within two weeks he secured three interviews and two job offers! Focus on your mental preparation, because if you do, what you're after will surely manifest itself in your outer world.

Firmly commit to achieving success. Do whatever it takes to ensure the best possible results when you are interviewed for the job. I will go into more detail about what to do later.

For now, because you've made a conscious and unconscious decision to be successful, you have transformed your outlook and given your job search purpose.

Remember, career success comes to those who keep moving. Now that you have focused first on your mental preparation, let's turn your attention to your physical preparation.

5 PHYSICAL PREPARATION

There are several key areas related to your physical preparation that you must pay attention to.

The Company

Oftentimes job hunters forget or overlook the importance of performing their due diligence, i.e., researching the company. Don't let that be you! You want to put your best foot forward. You want the interviewer to know that you are invested in _their_ success. Take the following preparatory steps to demonstrate your commitment.

Use all your resources to ensure that you know the basics about the company. Go to their website. See if they have a Facebook fan page and _Like_ it! Look for their tweets on Twitter. Check them out on Linkedin. A few simple Internet searches will usually yield more than enough information about the company and its mission. This simple step will help in your preparation when asked about how you heard about their company or what you know about their company.

Here's a homework assignment: Learn as much as you can about your potential employer. Use this list as a guide and find out everything you can about them.

- Company Name
- Company Website

- Facebook Fan Page
- Twitter Account Name
- LinkedIn Name
- Company Mission Statement
- How Long in Business
- Products and/or Services
- Key Personnel & Titles
- Number of Employees
- Office Locations
- Office Location Specialties
- Community Involvement
- Why they need a **DOCTR**

The acronym **DOCTR** means:
- **D**evelopment and direction: What's on the drawing board? What direction is the company headed? What's their five-year plan?
- **O**penings: Based on the company's mission and culture, how can you optimize your skills and abilities and show them how you can help them achieve their goals?
- **C**omplications and challenges: What's holding them back from achieving their goals? Is it talent, execution, lack of a plan, etc.?
- **T**iming: Show them why *now* is the best time to hire *you*.
- **R**elatable skills: What are your skills and talents? How can those specific and relatable skills best serve the organization?

This step will assist you in developing a clear mental snapshot of who they are and what they do. Make a note of the names of the executive leadership team. While it might take some clicking and digging, I cannot overemphasize the need to research, research, research!

Your Physical Appearance

You want to look the part of the successfully employed. Remember Anthony? To use another cliché, after getting out of his mental fog, when he went on the interview he dressed for success! You, too, must dress for success! It's true that you only have one time to make a favorable impression. It's also true that people do judge books by their covers—it might not be fair, nevertheless, it is true! Job interviewers pay close attention to the physical appearance of their applicants, namely the way they are dressed. Therefore, you should pay attention as well! Consider these four key points when preparing your physical appearance:

Be clean. You can show your potential employer how professional you really are if you are smart in your appearance and appropriately dressed for the position.

Be conservative. Even if conservative is not your style, remember it's more acceptable to people of all ages, cultures, and backgrounds. After all, you want acceptance into the company. I am compelled to include this word of caution here. If you have a friend that works for the company you are applying to work for, and you know your friend goes to work in jeans and a tee-shirt, you still need to dress for an interview! Save the casual dress for when you have the job!

What about tattoos and body piercings? Diane Gottsman, owner of The Protocol School of Texas, a company specializing in corporate etiquette training says this: "When a college student or young adult is interviewing for a job, a tattoo can make an unfavorable impression, even if the impression is not verbalized." I suggest my clients cover up the tattoos, remove the tongue rings, nose rings, etc. Gottsman agrees and posits, "In ten years, maybe the issue of body art won't be an issue worth discussing when it comes to human resources but for now, the Millennials who are seeking to expand the definition of professionalism still have to deal with the existing attitudes at many workplaces. The bottom line is that employers have a right to require their employees to dress in a manner that upholds the professionalism of the company."

You may be thinking it is a violation of your personal rights for a company to expect you to cover your tattoos and remove your jewelry; however, as of this writing, it is not considered discriminatory if companies refuse to allow employees to display body piercings and/or tattoos. Remember, as Gottsman warns, "When it comes down to it, if a company is deciding between two applicants, and one is visibly tattooed or pierced, they will most likely go for the non-tattooed and unpierced applicant.

Be free. Take care to avoid extreme hairstyles, clothes, make-up, and jewelry.

Be professional. Let your prospective employer know—through your professional appearance—that the job is important to you. You want your appearance to convey your seriousness, and your professionalism.

For Women:

Wear a dress, a business suit, or a pant suit. Make a good impression and choose something stylish, yet a bit on the conservative side.

Think about wearing knee-length skirts instead of full-length skirts. Yes, full-length skirts may be fashionable, but they are not appropriate for an interview.

If you can, get your hair done and get a manicure. If you cannot afford it, at least make sure that your hair is clean and nicely styled, and that your nails are clean and clipped.

For Men:

Wear a nice suit. If you don't have a nice suit, wear a dark pair of dress pants and a nice shirt and tie.

If you can, make an appointment with your barber! Remember, Men, just like women, you should pay attention to your hair and nails.

Shine your shoes! (Guys, this is extremely important. I remember visiting a neurosurgeon's office with my mom and the first thing I looked at was his shoes. They were scuffed, old, and beat-up. He lost every ounce of credibility with me and I made a mental note that we would not use his services again. Even though the degrees on his wall indicated he was a professional medical doctor, his shoes said he was slovenly, unkempt, and did not care about his appearance; consequently, in my eyes he probably didn't care about his patients either!)

I guarantee you will be pleasantly surprised at how much more confident you will feel just from implementing these simple steps! Remember, when you feel good about how you look, you will project a higher level of confidence that can help you nail your next job interview!

Other Common-Sense Considerations

Arrive 10 – 15 minutes early. Don't get there too early, though. I meet Human Resource personnel in my seminars all the time and they tell me that if a person gets there too early, it's just as bad as getting there late! Why? You're not respecting their time. They set the appointment planning on meeting with you for a specific amount of time. They're not expecting you an hour before the interview is scheduled.

Show your potential employer that you can follow instructions, that you are punctual, and that you care about their time as well as yours. If you do get there too early, don't go inside! Wait in the car, go get your favorite non-alcoholic beverage, and focus on having a positive interview. How? Pull out your written and vocal affirmations, do some deep breathing, and get your mind right!

Double-check the address. If you're driving and will be using your GPS, go online first to verify the address. I cannot tell you how many times I've put an address in my GPS and the GPS couldn't find it because the City recently renamed the street or the actual address was South Portland and not Portland!

It's also important to know if you have to pay for parking, especially if you're in a major metropolitan city like Atlanta or Manhattan. If you have to take public transportation, make sure you have the route and the schedule down pat. Whether you're driving or using public transportation, go the day before so that you are comfortable with the time it takes. You don't want any travel glitches on your big day!

Use your cell phone wisely. Put the company's address, phone number, and the name of your interviewer in the memo section of your phone. You can also use the recorder. If you have a Smartphone, iPhone, or iPad, there's probably an app you can download! The point is to make sure you can let someone know if circumstances beyond your control are making you late. Don't forget to turn your phone off after you arrive. It's rude and unacceptable to have your cell phone vibrating, beeping, singing, or ringing! If someone needs to reach you because of a pending family emergency, explain that to the interviewer up front. Better yet, if possible, tend to those situations before or after the interview.

When you get there, be polite to everyone you see! Your mom and dad were right when they told you that "please" and "thank you," go a long way! If the receptionist thinks you're rude and impolite, no matter how great your interview, it could cost you the job!

Take an emergency copy of your resume or Curriculum Vitae. You may have to use it in the interview because the interviewer does not have your packet in front of her. If she's pitch-hitting for another person, she will appreciate your thoughtfulness and attention to detail!

Self-Assessment

Here's another homework assignment. You want to impress your potential employer; right? You can do so if you prepare a script and practice before the actual interview. Get a notebook or use your computer for this exercise. From your resume, create a list of all the skills you have used for each past job.

Past Job	Skills Required to Perform the Job

Next, compile a list of your skills and strengths. This list should include personal traits, knowledge-based and transferable skills.

INTERVIEW SKILLS: HOW TO GET HIRED NOW!

My Personal Strengths	My Knowledge-Based Skills	My Portable Skills

You will use your lists to help you create your USP: Unique Selling Proposition. Give it some serious thought and answer these questions:

- Why should they hire you?
- What makes you unique?
- What makes you the best choice to fill this position?

Once you've completed your lists and answered the questions, you can craft a script using the AIDA formula, a formula used in the marketing industry:

Attention: Here's what I know about your organization.
Interest: These are the skills and this is my experience that will benefit you and your organization.
Desire: As we discuss my skills and experience, it will be a great idea for you to hire me.
Action: Hire me.

Working through the skills worksheets, and creating an AIDA script means you will be better prepared for your upcoming interview. Your potential employer wants to know what you have accomplished over the course of your career. It is important that you include all of your skills, both technical and non-technical. Remember, non-technical skills account for 80 percent of your success; consequently, you will want to highlight your leadership skills, communication skills, problem-solving skills, team building skills, etc.

Perfect Practice

Coach Vince Lombardi once said, "Practice does not make perfect. Only perfect practice makes perfect." Do yourself a favor and work on your interviewing skills before the interview. Most job seekers invest a great deal of time in creating the perfect resume, and neglect putting in as much time preparing for the actual interview. Remember, the interview is not the place to practice because you'll only have one opportunity to get this right.

While doing research for this guide I asked 20 people if they had ever practiced interviewing for a job, and only four (or 20 percent) said they had. Another interesting tidbit about that 20 percent—they enjoyed higher salaries than the 80 percent! While this was certainly no scientific study, I suspect that it is fairly accurate and highlights the importance of practice.

So, what should you practice during your practice sessions? I advise my coaching clients to focus on five basic areas, and I'm advising you to do the same.

1. Focus on how to answer questions
2. Focus on how you look when you answer questions
3. Focus on how you should look when you answer questions
4. Focus on how you sound when you answer questions
5. Focus on how you should sound when you answer questions

Conservatively, you should spend at least two to three hours in a mock interview session. If you can, record (video and audio) your practice sessions, and pay close attention to the words you've chosen to use, your tone of voice, and your body language. People make value judgments based on what they hear, see, and intuitively perceive. You want to make sure that your vocal, visual, and verbal cues are in harmony!

Consider hiring a professional to help you with the mock interview process. Companies such as jobinterviewedge.com specialize in preparing you for the actual interview using a mock interview. Mock interviewing will help you gain confidence, reduce interview angst, and give you that all important edge. I have listed a few of the top companies who provide this service in the Appendix. You can also contact me at: http://www.drangelamassey.com and I will coach you.

6 NOW THAT YOU'RE IN

Okay. You look good, you feel good, you're in the interviewer's office, now what? Here are a few tips I teach in my communication seminars that I would like to share with you to help you make a great first impression:

Make and maintain good eye contact. However, don't stare! Look the interviewer in the eyes and hold contact for about three seconds. Experts tell us that the person who makes and maintains eye contact demonstrates self-confidence. On the contrary, the person who fails to make and maintain good eye contact unknowingly demonstrates a lack of trust, or a short attention span.

Greet the interviewer with a firm handshake. Don't squeeze too hard and don't allow your hand to be too limp! Consider the findings of a handshake study conducted by The University of Alabama and published in the July 2000 issue of the Journal of Personality and Social Psychology, a journal published by the American Psychological Association: "Those with a firm handshake were more extroverted and open to experience and less neurotic and shy than those with a less firm or limp handshake."

Flash your best smile with your friendliest greeting! Why? According to research, optimistic job seekers are more likely to get hired! Additionally, smiling helps to reduce and even alleviate the stress often related to interviewing.

Wait for direction. Once you're in the interviewer's office, sit only when you are asked to do so. This subtle move speaks volumes in terms of respect!

Before the interview starts, thank the interviewer for taking time to interview you. This allows you to start the interview on a positive note.

Presenting Your Work History

Your career history is an essential element in the interview. Generally mentioned immediately after the customary chit-chat of whether you experienced challenges trying to find the office, comments related to weather conditions, etc., the interviewer zooms in asking for details about your past employment experiences.

A comprehensive resume identifying noteworthy results in your previous positions will spark the discussion. Now is your opportunity to elaborate on those results. For example, substantially growing revenue in the sales department by 23.8% each quarter or shrinking the budget by 14.5% because you led a retail reorganization are the kinds of results that deserve elaboration. Clearly, these kinds of achievements as pointed out within your CV or resume propelled the prospective employer to contact you and schedule this interview. So don't be shy! Toot your horn. The interviewer expects you to give her the particulars and the details connected with the steps you performed to get such fantastic results.

Unfortunately, most people do the kind of job in which the outcomes are not quite so apparent. Assuming you have worked in manufacturing or perhaps customer service or even retail, it is extremely challenging to link your time and efforts directly to business results. When this happens, try to focus on any specific individualized successes or organizational recognition that will demonstrate your proficiency.

Any kind of advancement is excellent, despite the fact that it may have been no more than to a lead position or just being put in control of a unique task. Talk about what you accomplished so that the interviewer can recognize the value of your prior employer's belief in your capability to tackle new responsibilities.

Perhaps you did not advance in your position—sometimes there are no options for advancement—simply pinpoint any situations where your contributions were acknowledged with favorable recognition. That covers anything from having been requested to teach new colleagues that new software program to getting a free day off because you were chosen staffer of the month for the incredible customer service you provided on the Jenkins account.

If superiors made positive comments about you and your work ethic, describe the facts to the interviewer. While every job candidate attempts to show themselves as Mr. or Ms. Absolute Best Worker Ever, the fact remains that a lot of us work extremely hard for years without ever getting a legitimate promotion or even very much acknowledgement. Employers know that. Believe it or not, if the position is routine with little opportunity for upward mobility, for example, a receptionist position, they may be cautious with Ms. Absolute Best Worker if she jokes about the insufficient advancement possibilities. While it's unfair, but true, if Ms. Absolute Best Worker has a PhD and she is looking for employment as a receptionist, she would definitely be viewed with suspicion.

If you are Mr. Absolute Best Worker ever—that is, you have a solid work background (just void of promotions or advancement), highlight and describe in the detail your strongest assets. For example, perhaps you hardly ever called in sick, or enjoyed a track record for punctuality or even getting to meetings before time; this is your opportunity to shine the spotlight on your strengths.

For those of you who have spent 5, 10, or even 20 years working for just one employer, your challenge during this part of the interview is to show the interviewer that you are flexible and adapt well to change. While she may not say it, she's concerned that you might be stuck in your ways, and could bring that obstinacy with you into a new work environment. Here you want to stress your versatility and desire to learn new tasks. If you were cross-trained and transferred between departments or had a job title change or your duties increased throughout your lengthy tenure, provide the particulars and let the interviewer know how adaptable you are.

In case your work history is varied with a good deal of jobs for brief amounts of time, explain just how much you acquired as a result of each individual position. Be sure to point out your eagerness to combine all that you've learned and all of your work encounters into one established profession. Express your diligence in your search for an organization (such as the one you're interviewing with right now) specifically where you can stabilize your career and commit to the organization and yourself.

I cannot emphasize this enough. Before going into this process, take some time to analyze and document the numerous facets connected with your own work background that offer an optimistic twist. I said this earlier in this chapter: toot your own horn! You needn't be afraid to focus on your positive traits in spite of how unimpressive you think your prior positions were.

7 THE NUTS AND BOLTS OF THE INTERVIEW

The interview is probably the most difficult part for most people because there is always apprehension about what questions will be asked, and the appropriate responses to those questions. This is where your emotional intelligence comes into play.

How you answer the job interview questions will determine if you are hired. You cannot prepare too much in this area, and for that reason I've listed some standard questions and suggested answers. Remember to make the answers your own.

One final thought on this—the best way to answer job interview questions is honestly and directly. To adequately prepare yourself for competency-based questions designed to ascertain your emotional intelligence, download a copy of my ebook: *Interview Questions: How to Answer CORRECTLY!*

Standard Interview Questions You May Be Asked

Example question: *How would you describe yourself?*

Your answer should describe qualities that will clearly illustrate why you are the right person for the position. If you've done the homework prescribed in earlier chapters you will be able to answer this question—no problem!

Example question: *What are your long-term goals?*

Your answer should be based on your career goals—both short- and long-term. What do you want to be when you grow up? Make sure you have your goals written down and that you are ready to discuss them. Again, if you did the work in an earlier chapter, the answer to this question will flow easily.

Example question: *Why did you leave your last job?*

Your answer could be for more responsibility, a better opportunity, or increased income. Whatever you say, be certain to avoid this faux pas: Under no circumstances are you to speak negatively of your previous employer, even if your previous employer was horrible! Consider this advice printed in the Chicago Tribune by Carol Kleiman: "Acing a job interview is not about feeling good. It's about getting the job. If you pour out all your emotions on these poor, unsuspecting people, it will only make you appear disloyal and difficult to get along with. And no one wants to hire anyone like that." It reflects poorly on you, and will cause your potential employer to wonder if you would do the same thing to him.

Example question: *Why do you want this job?*

Your answer should be that you want more responsibility or better opportunity or something similar. Avoid mentioning anything personal, e.g., this location is close to my child's day care, or I can stop in at the YWCA on my way home to exercise.

Example question: *What are your strengths?*

Your answer should highlight accomplishments and experiences that relate to the position for which you are applying. Remember the list I mentioned in a previous chapter:

- Problem solving
- Leadership leader potential
- Organizational skills
- Excellent writing and communication skills

- Customer service oriented
- Able to effectively manage time and projects
- Critical thinker

Use this list as a basis to highlight your accomplishments and experiences. Also, give examples of situations where your strengths have been demonstrated.

Example question: *What are your weaknesses?*

Your answer should not be a list of your deficiencies. Don't mention anything that could make the interviewer question your ability to do the job, for example "I am always late for everything." Instead, discuss a weakness that could also be a strength such as "I am a workaholic!"

I like this advice from Paul Michael, Senior Writer for wisebread.com: "If you're completely honest, you may be kicking yourself in the butt. If you say you don't have one, you're obviously lying. This is a horrible question and one that politicians have become masters at answering. They say things like "I'm perhaps too committed to my work and don't spend enough time with my family." Oh, there's a fireable offense. I've even heard "I think I'm too good at my job, it can often make people jealous." Please, let's keep our feet on the ground. If you're asked this question, give a small, work-related flaw that you're working hard to improve. Example: "I've been told I occasionally focus on details and miss the bigger picture, so I've been spending time laying out the complete project every day to see my overall progress."

Example question: *Tell me a little bit about yourself.*

Your answer should include information about your current position. If you're not working, focus on your most recent position. Since this question is primarily asked to set the stage for the interview, I caution you to be careful in how you answer it! Stay away from elaborating on your life. Rather, talk about the relevant facts regarding your education, your career, and your current life situation.

Example question: *What made you want to make this change?*

Your answer should reflect that you have done some research about the company and you've given some thought to why working for this organization would be a great opportunity.

Sage advice from Carole Martin, Contributing Writer for Monster.com: "...think of at least two reasons this job is a good match for your skills, strengths, experience, and background. What can you bring to the company? Write down your thoughts and rehearse them as part of your script. ...Your answer should reflect that you have thought about what you want and have researched the company. Let the interviewer know you are being selective about where you want to work and you're not just going to take any job offered to you. Demonstrate that this is the company you want to work for—a little flattery will go a long way."

Example question: *What do you most enjoy doing in your current or most recent position?*

Your answer should focus on tangible accomplishments and achievements in your current job (or recent position if you're unemployed right now). Here's what I mean: "I really enjoyed working on a team where I was able to positively influence the way we met our goals. It was extremely satisfying to help lead my co-workers to accomplish the goals set by our manager, especially under a tight deadline."

Example question: *Describe your future ambitions.*

Your answer should reflect that you have concrete and well-thought out plans for your future, and how this potential job fits into those plans. Explain your career goals and objectives.

The interviewer wants to know if you are established, and if you're not, she wants to know that you are planning to do so. She wants you to tell her in detail how you have planned ahead, both professionally and personally. Remember, be honest and realistic. Don't be afraid to show a high level of enthusiasm about reaching your goals. After all, this is your life you're talking about!

<u>Example question:</u> *How would you describe yourself?*

Your answer should start with a question! This advice comes from a recruiter (and who knows better than a recruiter, right?): "…say, 'I will gladly answer that question, but may I first ask you a question?'" The recruiter goes on to say, "(They ALWAYS say yes) So that I may better focus my answer, what are the issues you want me to address should you hire me?" Once they share with you what they need to have you do, then proceed to address how your training, education, skills, and experience can best resolve these issues. By answering in this fashion, you have proven that you know how to focus. Most importantly, you have also shown that you have what's needed to fix the issues they need to have fixed.

You do not take on impossible workloads.

A manager has to maintain a productive, positive tone even when she's anxious about a business threat. How have you been able to do this in previous positions? Your answer should reflect that:

You stay composed under pressure.
You remain calm, confident, and dependable—in the heat of crises.
You orchestrate win-win solutions.

High performers understand the need to work with and through others. They can accurately interpret other people's emotions and discern their opinions. Additionally, top performers with high EQ can read others' cues and adjust their own words and behaviors accordingly. To assess your skill level in this aspect of emotional intelligence, the interviewer may ask this type of EI-based question:

Tell me about a time when you did or said something that had a negative impact on a customer, peer, or direct report. How did you know the impact was negative? Your answer should reflect that:

You paid attention to the person's body language and behavior.
You adjusted your behavior based on what you noticed about the other person.
You did not ask, "What's wrong?" Rather, you relied on your ability to read people and situations—you didn't get someone else involved to point out the error of your ways or the correctness of your actions.

Moral: Your answers to emotional intelligence-based questions will make the difference!

9 QUESTIONS YOU MAY ASK

Customarily at the end of the interview the interviewer will ask if you have any questions. Be prepared with a few questions to show your interest in the position as well as the company. Remember, not asking questions may be interpreted as you not being interested in the job or the company. Stay away from questions regarding salary, benefits, insurance, etc. Naturally you want to know about these things; however, now is not the time to ask. After all, you do not want your potential employer to think that you're only interested in what he can do for you.

In his famous book *The Seven Habits of Highly Effective People* Dr. Stephen Covey stresses the importance of proactivity labeling it the second habit of an highly effective person. Covey said, "If you're proactive, you don't have to wait for circumstances or people to create perspective expanding experiences. You can consciously create your own." Simply put, in the context of your interview, prepare, and rehearse at least five questions to ask that clearly establish your interest in and your desire to be a part of the organization. Here are a few guidelines to help you craft great questions to ask the interviewer:

Ask questions that show you were paying attention. For example, "You mentioned earlier that the company is rolling out a new software system. Please tell me more about that."

Ask questions that show you know something about the organization and its mission. For example, "According to my research about XYZ

Corporation part of the company's mission is to be the finest premier furniture store in the country; tell me how your department contributes to the overall mission."

If the interviewer mentioned organizational changes and/or challenges, don't be afraid to ask him to clarify. Additionally, you can use this time to show your expertise in a certain area, i.e. you've been following the trend on Facebook that suggests companies need to place more emphasis on social media marketing. This information posed as a question will allow you to show your concern about the company's marketing efforts or lack thereof.

Many interviewees overlook this golden opportunity to position themselves as a valuable future member of the organization's team. Remember, asking questions at the end of the interview has three benefits:

1. You will gain valuable information about the organization and the job you applied for.
2. You will increase your likability factor.
3. You will stand out as a candidate interested in the position and the organization.

After scouring tons of website and reading numerous books, I have compiled a list of great questions you may want to consider as you prepare for your interview.

General Questions

- What are the most important skills and attributes a candidate needs to be successful in this position?
- What are the characteristics of a successful employee in your organization?
- Describe the work environment.
- What are the challenging facets of the job?
- What would be a typical work day in this position?
- What is your management style?

- What is your preferred method of communicating with your team?
- What is the next step in the interviewing process?

Company Culture

- How would you describe your company culture?
- What is the organizational structure of your department?
- Who are the primary parties that you are responsible to support: shareholders, customers, employees, etc.?
- How do you go about making decisions when the needs of these groups are at odds with each other?

Measures for Success

- What are your expectations for new employee hires within their first 90 days on the job? Within the first six months?
- How and when will my job performance be evaluated?
- What metrics are used to measure whether or not you are achieving your predetermined goals?
- How will my success in this position be measured?
- How is success measured in this department (or organization)?

The Future of the Organization

- How and when will my job performance be evaluated?
- What is your vision for the organization (or department) over the next two years? Next five years?
- What current major challenges are you facing as a manager?
- What is the organization's biggest challenge currently?
- What is the organization's competitive advantage in the marketplace?

10 DUH…HOW TO GET UNSTUMPED IF YOU GET STUMPED BY A QUESTION

In this chapter let's take a look at three problematic areas as they relate to interview questions:

1. You are asked an off-the-wall question.
2. You experience a momentary memory lapse.
3. You are speechless as to how to answer the question.

The Off-The-Wall Question

Every now and again an interviewer may ask you a question that has absolutely nothing to do with the position you are interviewing for (or so it seems). Consider these crazy questions asked by real companies:

"What was your best MacGyver moment?" An interviewer at Schlumberger, the giant Houston oilfield services provider, asked this question.

"If you were a brick in a wall, which brick would you be and why?" An interviewer at Nestlé USA asked this question.

"How would you move Mt. Fuji?" An interviewer at Microsoft asked this question.

"How many hair salons are there in Japan?" An interviewer at Boston Consulting asked this question.

Did you notice what I said earlier about a question that seems like it has nothing to do with the position? During an interview with Forbes writer Susan Adams, Rusty Rueff—former head of human resources at PepsiCo, stated that, "Ninety percent of people don't know how to deal with them [off-the-wall interview questions]."

Rueff gives some very valuable advice regarding these kinds of questions. While it might feel like the interviewer is trying to make you look stupid, realize that is not the purpose of the question. For instance, Rueff advises "the MacGyver question is meant just as an invitation to talk about how you got out of a tough jam."

If you are under the age of 25, a reference to MacGyver probably wouldn't even make sense! Rueff goes on to say, "They're not looking for you to tell about the time you took out your ballpoint and did a tracheotomy." If you've done your homework and prepared for the interview, you should be able to relate how you still got the job done and achieved a positive result without all of the necessary tools and support. By the way, *MacGyver* (a TV show that aired 1985 – 1992) was a secret agent able to solve crimes, outwit the enemy, and keep his hair in place—all while only using a Swiss Army knife!

Here's another example Rueff talked with Ms. Adams about:
"What about a question like 'how many hair salons are there in Japan?' the interviewer is giving you an opportunity to demonstrate your thought processes." Rueff says you should think out loud, like the contestants on *Who Wants to Be a Millionaire?* You might start by saying, we have to know the population of Japan, and then we have to figure out what percentage of them get their hair done and how often. Rueff says it's fine to pull out a pen and paper and start doing some calculations right there in the interview."

Contrary to most of the information on the Internet, seemingly off-topic questions are not "thrown into the interview out of curiosity or to gauge your knowledge on a certain subject." Rather, these questions are designed to see how fast you think on your feet, to test your problem-solving abilities, and to determine if you can think outside of the lines. Even if you are not able to figure out the correlation between the question and the job you are interviewing for, remember to remain cool, calm, and collected. Take a deep breath, compose yourself and give the interviewer your best answer.

The Momentary Memory Lapse

There are two schools of thought on what I am about to say to you: Make it a habit to take a notepad and pen—not your iPad or iPhone!—with you to your interviews. Some experts say that you should never take a notepad and pen with you to an interview, while others say you should always do so. Of course, I will leave that decision up to you, but here's why I suggest it (especially if you're prone to become so nervous you experience a momentary memory lapse):

- You will project a certain level of professionalism that the average candidate does not think about.
- You will project a higher level of awareness about the organization and the position (You should have your notes handy!)
- You will prepare yourself for the next level of interviews because you will create a brief outline of what was discussed in this interview.

Be sure to let the interviewer know that you would like to jot down some notes—ask, don't tell. Aaron Wallis, a sales recruitment firm advise:

"Ask to take down notes—you'll get a 'brownie point' for being polite, let them subtly see the research that you have undertaken in preparation for the meeting. Invest in a document case where you can have your pad on the right side and your interview questions and even a list of your strengths and aspirations to the left side. When you get that tough question—a quick dart down to your left and you'll be back on track."

You Become Speechless As to How to Answer a Question

First, should you become speechless because you are not sure what kind of answer the interviewer is looking for, simply ask him to explain his question. Try asking for an example and listen for an indication as to what he is really looking for.

Second, here's a hot tip I teach in my public speaking classes which can be applied to a momentary memory lapse or being speechless: take a bottle of water with you or ask for a glass of water right before the interview starts. In those few precious seconds where you either forget or don't know what to say, take a drink of water. This will give you time to formulate a reasonable response. As with the entire interview process, the key to the most effective way to respond is honestly.

11 WHAT'S NEXT?

I mentioned at the beginning of this book that you are responsible for letting your potential employer know what makes you the more qualified candidate for the job you are interviewing for.

During the process, make sure that your potential employer has a real sense of who you are and the skills, talents, and abilities you possess. He should know why hiring you is his best and only choice! Exude confidence even if you're short on experience. I had a boss at IBM who used to say, "I'd rather have a bunch of thoroughbreds that I have to pull back than a bunch of asses I have to kick!" Demonstrate you eagerness to learn and grow.

Now that the interview is over, take a few minutes to summarize your strengths. Remind the interviewer that you are the person for the job. Last, but certainly not least, thank him for his time and his consideration of you as a candidate.

Once you get home remember to write a thank you note. The operative word here is "write." I know it is easy with today's technology to send a quick e-mail or even a text message. However, an old-fashioned thank you note will go far to impress the interviewer and help you stand out from other job candidates with similar experience, education, and background. Today's current job market is competitive, and you must do all you can to make sure that you make the best impression. Why send a thank you note?

- It will make you stand out.
- It will get you noticed.
- It will give you an opportunity to reiterate your interest in the position.
- It will give you a chance to mention something you may have forgotten.

Compile a list of every person's name involved in the interview: HR personnel, managers, and support staff. Pay special attention to the spelling of each name. Jot down something unique to that person. For example, perhaps Jennifer, the administrative assistant that set up the interview was extremely polite and kind. Maybe she took the time to give you detailed directions. Your personalized thank-you to her might look something like this: "Jennifer, thank you for taking the time to give me directions to ABC Corporation. As you know I interviewed with Mr. Brown today, and it meant a lot to me to be able to get to ABC Corporation on time and stress free. It's easy to see that ABC Corporation hires only the best!"

Your thank you note to Mr. Brown might look something like this: "Dear Mr. Brown, thank you again for taking the time to interview me this afternoon for the assistant manager position with ABC Corporation. My interview with you underscores my desire to be a part of the ABC Corporation team, and I'm positive that employment with ABC Corporation would be a win-win for the company and for me."

Karen Schweitzer, Business School Guide for About.com, also advises:

"If you are handwriting the note, use nice stationary or a card and write neatly. If typing the note, be sure to include a legible signature at the bottom.

Make an effort to avoid sounding mechanical and obligatory. If sending several notes, try to make each one original. And finally, be sure to send the thank-you note no later than one day after your interview."

Remember, a good thank-you note/letter gets to the point. It should be short, simple, and savvy. It was your great resume that got you the job interview. It was your commitment to detail and preparation that made the interview great. It will be your effective thank-you note/letter that seals the deal and get you what you want—HIRED NOW!

APPENDIX

I've done all the work for you! Here's a list of resources (along with a key indicating if the resource is free or not) to help you find and get that job. The list is categorized in the typical sequential steps job-seekers take: Resumes, Cover Letters, Interviewing, and Thank-You Letters/Notes. *Please note at the time of this publication, all links worked. If you try a link and it does not work, let me know so that I can update my list.* Enjoy!

Resumes

Books or Kindle Books
- *Resumes for Dummies* by Joyce Lain Kennedy
- *The 21st Century Resume Guide For The Perplexed* by Mary Elizabeth Bradford
- *The Resume.Com Guide to Writing Unbeatable Resumes* by Rose Curtis
- *Knock 'm Dead Resumes: Features the Latest Information on: Online Posting, Email Techniques, and Follow-up Strategies* by Martin Yate
- *The Twitter Job Search Guide: Find a Job and Advance Your Career in Just 15 Minutes a Day* by Susan Britton Whitcomb
- *The Resume Handbook: How to Write Outstanding Resumes and Cover Letters for Every Situation* by Arthur Rosenberg and David V. Hizer
- *How to Write Powerful College Student Resumes and Cover Letters: Secrets That Get Job Interviews Like Magic* by Quentin J. Schultze
- *What Color Is Your Parachute? 2012: A Practical Manual for Job-Hunters and Career-Changers* by Richard N. Bolles
- *The Job-Hunter's Survival Guide: How to Find a Reward Job Even When "There Are No Jobs"* by Richard N. Bolles

YouTube Videos

- Basic Resume Creation:
http://www.youtube.com/watch?v=tona4OD0E0Q&feature=related
- Beginner Resume Builder:
http://www.youtube.com/watch?v=zAKGr09d3JE&feature=related
- How to Write a Powerful Resume to Get a Job Fast:
http://www.youtube.com/watch?v=kXAyqizRBuU&feature=related
- Resumes for Young People with no Experience:
- http://www.youtube.com/watch?v=cpM4EOhHibM&feature=related
- Building Your Resume as a Student:
http://www.youtube.com/watch?v=_u4tcFA6SG4&feature=related
- Top Ten Resume Mistakes: http://www.youtube.com/watch?v=PeZ-cIPGtLc&feature=related

On-line Courses and/or Software
($) http://www.universalclass.com/i/course/resume-writing-tutorial.htm
($) http://www.ed2go.com/online-courses/resume-writing-workshop.html
(FREE)
http://www.openlearningworld.com/innerpages/Resume%20Writing.htm
(FREE) http://owl.english.purdue.edu/owl/resource/719/1/
(FREE W/STIPULATIONS)
http://career.ucla.edu/Students/Workshops/OnlineResumeWritingWorkshop.aspx/
(FREE) http://resumizer.com/
($) http://www.howtowritearesume.net/
($) http://www.resumetemplates.org/
($) http://www.livecareer.com/
($) http://www.blueskyresumes.com/our-services/resume-writing-course/
($) http://resume-now.com/rna.aspx
($)
http://resumecompanion.com/?gclid=CMrbyfPlh60CFcNo4AoddQEDmA
($) http://resume-builder.net/

Apps for iPhone, iPad, iTouch, iTunes
(FREE) ReSuM8 by Career Marketing Specialists Inc.:
http://itunes.apple.com/us/app/resum8/id468624825?mt=8
($) Resume App by Vurgood Applications:
http://itunes.apple.com/us/app/resume-app/id313779951?mt=8
($) Resume Rockstar by Minervaz: http://itunes.apple.com/us/app/resume-rockstar/id396841009?mt=8
($) ResumeBase by abovehorizon.com:
http://itunes.apple.com/us/app/resumebase/id467902809?mt=8

($) ResumeRight by jchaike Creations:
http://itunes.apple.com/us/app/resumeright/id352213736?mt=8

Apps for Androids
($) Pocket Resume by Mani Ghasemlou:
http://www.androidzoom.com/android_applications/business/pocket-resume_bdwim.html
(FREE) Best Resume Tips by RJF:
http://www.androidzoom.com/android_applications/books_and_reference/best-resume-tips_qoxn.html
(FREE) RezScore by RezScore.com:
http://www.androidzoom.com/android_applications/productivity/rezscore_blbga.html

Blogs on Resume Writing
http://www.gotthejob.com/blog/
http://ladybug-design.com/blog/
http://www.blueskyresumes.com/blog/
http://www.effortlesshr.com/blog/employee-hiring/top-ten-tips-resume-writing/

Cover Letters

Books or Kindle Books
- *Career Essentials: The Cover Letter* by Dale Mayer
- *No-Nonsense Cover Letters: The Essential Guide to Creating Attention-Grabbing Cover Letters That Get Interviews & Job Offers (No-Nonsense)* by Wendy S. Enelow and Arnold G. Boldt
- *Cover Letters for Dummies* by Joyce Lain Kennedy
- *The Elements of Resume Style: Essential Rules and Eye-Opening Advice for Writing Resumes and Cover Letters that Work* by Scott Bennett
- *15-Minute Cover Letter: Write an Effective Cover Letter Right Now (15 Minute Cover Letter)* by Michael Farr and Louise M. Kursmark
- *Winning Cover Letters* by Robin Ryan
- *How to Find a Job: When There Are No Jobs, 2012 Edition: A Necessary Job Search Book for Surviving and Prospering in Today's Hyper Competitive Job Market* by Paul Rega

INTERVIEW SKILLS: HOW TO GET HIRED NOW!

On-line Tutorials
- Dynamic Cover Letters Tutorial For Developing a Stunningly Effective Cover Letter: http://www.quintcareers.com/cover_letter_tutorial.html
- Cover Letter Tutorial: http://www.uidaho.edu/careercenter/Students/Cover%20Letters/Cover%20Letter%20Tutorial
- Cover Letter Tutorial: http://www.umuc.edu/students/support/careerservices/coverlettertutorial.cfm
- Cover Letter Tutorial: http://www.eduers.com/resume/Cover_Letter_Tutorial.htm

Youtube Videos
- Writing the Perfect Cover Letter: http://www.youtube.com/watch?v=oiR3Uu5sbXw&feature=related
- Tips to Write an Effective Cover Letter for a Job: http://www.youtube.com/watch?v=auRcak_ibSk&feature=related
- Cover Letter Format: http://www.youtube.com/watch?v=JbrMqcdjC9M&feature=related
- Job Application Cover Letter: http://www.youtube.com/watch?v=Q4XCn4VLfM8&feature=related
- Cover Letters Sample: http://www.youtube.com/watch?v=WcjgpZm7aSk&feature=related

Interview Skills

Books or Kindle Books
- *301 Smart Answers to Tough Interview Questions* by Vicki Oliver
- *How to Answer Hard Interview Questions* by Charlie Gibbs
- *101 Great Answers to the Toughest Interview Questions* by Ron Fly
- *201 Knockout Answers to Interview Questions* by Linda Matias
- *Competency-Based Interviews* by Ron Kessler
- *Acing the Interview* by Tony Beshara
- *Interview Questions: How to Answer Emotional Intelligence Questions to Get Your Next Job* by Angela D. Massey, PhD

Thank-You Letters

Books or Kindle Books

- *Interview Follow Up Guide for the Perplexed (the Career Artisan Series)* by Mary Elizabeth Bradford
- *How to Write Perfect Thank You Letters* by Don Georgevich

YouTube Videos

- How to Write a Sample Thank You Letter: http://www.youtube.com/watch?v=rYtWDVQpv7g
- How to Write a Thank You Note: http://www.youtube.com/watch?v=VjMmYGNXoaI&feature=related
- Job Interview Tips: How to Write a Thank-You Note After a Job Interview: http://www.youtube.com/watch?v=NIzMbVvGOws&feature=related
- Interview Tips – What to Do After Your Interview: http://www.youtube.com/watch?v=dct7MR1s6ug&feature=related

Mock Interviews

Website Addresses

- http://www.jobinterviewedge.com
- http://www.jobinterview-practice.com
- http://www.interviewgold.com
- http://www.statusnext.com

CITATIONS AND REFERENCES

- Brescia, Mike: http://www.thinkrightnow.com
- Covey, Stephen: https://www.stephencovey.com/7habits/7habits.php
- Dooly, Mike: Thoughts Become Things
- Gottsman, Diane: http://www.protocolschooloftexas.com/
- Hansen, Randall and Hansen, Katherine: http://www.Quintcareers.com
- Kleiman, Carol: Retired Chicago Tribune Writer
- Lynn, Adele B.: *The EQ Interview: Finding Employees with High Emotional Intelligence*
- Martin, Carole: http://www.monster.com
- Michael, Paul: http://www.wisebread.com
- Whitcomb-Britton, Susan*: Interview Magic*

ABOUT THE AUTHOR

Dr. Angela D. Massey is an international speaker, author, corporate trainer, and life coach. The owner of Life On Purpose LLC, "Dr. Angela" as she is affectionately called, travels throughout the U.S. and internationally empowering people to close the gaps keeping them from realizing their true success. She has delivered over 1,000 seminars, workshops, and keynotes in her career. You can visit her on the web at: http://www.drangelamassey.com

Dr. Angela has authored four books:

- *Going the Distance! Success Strategies for On-line Students*
- *101 Pearls of Purpose*
- *Interview Skills: How to Get Hired NOW! Quick Job Interview Success Tips*
- *Turbo-Charge Your Team*

Currently, she is working on her soon-to-be-released fifth book, *Interview Questions: How to Answer Emotional Intelligence Questions to Get Your Next Job.*

She lives in Connecticut, and is the proud mother of 3 adult children and Nana extraordinaire to her 6 adorable grandchildren: Julius, Andrew, Malachi, Hunter, Ja'el, and Cole.

WHAT PEOPLE ARE SAYING ABOUT INTERVIEW SKILLS: HOW TO GET HIRED NOW!

Great Book!

"I wish I would have known about this book a long time ago, because I could be in the career of my life right now!

Dr. Massey, put a great effort into writing this book. It's very helpful, informative, and true. I look forward to reading more books from Dr. Massey.

GREAT BOOK!"

This is a gem in its field!

"Dr Massey's first words are 'Congratulations ... they want you to come in for an interview.' And for the next 44 pages (Kindle ebook) she tells you how to win the job. You learn how to prepare for an interview; you learn how to conduct yourself during interview; you learn how you can sway an interviewer's opinion of you; and you learn what you should do to follow up an interview."

I got a lot of great tips from this book!

"This is an enjoyable read and absolutely packed with gems of wisdom to help make any job interview go much better. Your chances of getting hired will improve dramatically from the advice in this book. Beautifully written and sound information. In fact, even if you're not interviewing for work there are so many helpful tidbits that can be applied to everyday situations... this book will benefit everyone who reads it. Good for any type of relationship too. Loved it."

Very Informative!

(Attended a webinar based on the book) "It was very informative. Thank you!

Quite Valuable

"I found your information to be quite valuable, and I will be sure to implement it when I get the invitation to participate in an interview....hopefully soon"

WHAT PEOPLE ARE SAYING ABOUT DR. ANGELA!

"The tools you taught in this class (Management Skills) have become a part of my daily life...I have recommended your work to many of my colleagues and friends..."

"Loved the high energy of Angela and the valuable information provided."

"Angela was energetic, humorous, and knowledgeable! Bring her back."

Contact Dr. Angela D. Massey at
http://www.drangelamassey.com **to schedule a keynote, expert training session, or personal interview coaching.**

CPSIA information can be obtained at www.ICGtesting.com
Printed in the USA
LVOW101618191212

312426LV00002B/194/P